Biblical Foundation 8

What is the Church?

by Larry Kreider

House To House Publications
Lititz, Pennsylvania USA

What is the Church?

Larry Kreider

Updated Edition © 2002, Reprinted 2003, 2006
Copyright © 1993, 1997, 1999
House to House Publications
11 Toll Gate Road, Lititz, PA 17543
Telephone: 800.848.5892
Web site: www.dcfi.org

ISBN 1-886973-07-5
Design and illustrations by Sarah Sauder

C O N T E N T S

Books in this Series

This is the eighth book in a twelve-book series designed to help believers to build a solid biblical foundation in their lives.

A corresponding *Biblical Foundations for Children* book is also available (see page 63).

Introduction

The foundation of the Christian faith is built on Jesus Christ and His Word to us, the Holy Bible. This twelve-book *Biblical Foundation Series* includes elementary principles every Christian needs to help lay strong spiritual foundations in his or her life.

In this eighth Biblical Foundation book, *What is the Church?* we will see the importance of being a part of a spiritual family united under Christ. This spiritual family gives us a place to grow and learn from other believers how to live our Christian lives. We need this input from spiritual leaders and fellow believers. We need one another. We are not supposed to live the Christian life alone. God's will is for every believer to be connected to a local church where he can be trained, protected, and available to serve others.

In this book, the foundation truths from the Word of God are presented with modern day parables that help you easily understand the basics of Christianity. Use this book and the other 11 *Biblical Foundation* books to lay a solid spiritual foundation in your life, or if you are already a mature Christian, these books are great tools to assist you in discipling others. May His Word become life to you today.

God bless you!

Larry Kreider

How to Use This Resource

Personal study

Read from start to finish as an individual study program to build a firm Christian foundation and develop spiritual maturity.
- Each chapter has a key verse excellent to commit to memory.
- Additional scriptures in gray boxes are used for further study.
- Each reading includes questions for personal reflection and room to journal at the end of the book.

Daily devotional

Use as a devotional for a daily study of God's Word.
- Each chapter is divided into 7-day sections for weekly use.
- Additional days at the end of the book bring the total number of devotionals to one complete month. The complete set of 12 books gives one year's worth of daily devotionals.
- Additional scriptures are used for further study.
- Each day includes reflection questions and a place to write answers at the end of the book.

Mentoring relationship

Use for a spiritual parenting relationship to study, pray and discuss life applications together.
- A spiritual father or mother can easily take a spiritual son or daughter through these short Bible study lessons and use the reflection questions to provoke dialogue about what is learned.
- Read each day or an entire chapter at a time.

Small group study

Study this important biblical foundation in a small group setting.
- The teacher studies the material in the chapters and teaches, using the user-friendly outline provided at the end of the book.

Taught as a biblical foundation course

These teachings can be taught by a pastor or other Christian leader as a basic biblical foundation course.
- Students read an assigned portion of the material.
- In the class, the leader teaches the assigned material using the chapter outlines at the end of the book.

CHAPTER 1

The Importance of the Local Church

KEY MEMORY VERSE

And let us consider how we may spur one another on toward love and good deeds. Let us not give up meeting together, as some are in the habit of doing, but let us encourage one another—and all the more as you see the Day approaching.

Hebrews 10:24-25

We need each other

I once read the story of a young man who had given his life to God; but after a time of disappointment and disillusionment, he began to withdraw from other Christians. The young man's pastor stopped in for a visit one cold, blustery winter evening and with the wind howling outside, they sat and talked.

After awhile, the wise pastor walked over to the fireplace, and with a pair of prongs picked up a hot coal from the fire, placing it on the bricks in front of the fireplace. He continued to converse with the young man. Then glancing at the ember on the bricks, he said, "Do you see that piece of coal? While it was in the fireplace it burned brightly, but now that it's alone, the ember has almost gone out."

The pastor walked over to the fireplace, and with the prongs, picked up the ember and placed it inside the fireplace. Within minutes, the dying ember was again burning brightly.

It suddenly dawned on the young man what the pastor was trying to tell him. When we move away from the warmth and encouraging fires of fellow believers in the body of Christ, we will eventually cool down spiritually. Joining with others as a community of believers in a local church body helps keep our fires glowing. From that day on, the young man made a decision to join regularly with other believers in a local church in his community. He did not want to take the chance of his fire going out again.

The Bible says in Hebrews 3:13, *But encourage one another daily, as long as it is called Today, so that none of you may be hardened by sin's deceitfulness*. It is extremely difficult to live the Christian life alone. Believers need to fellowship together and encourage one another daily because it is easy to become increasingly tolerant of sin in our lives otherwise.

A friend of mine once said, "Lone Rangers often get shot out of the saddle." He was referring to the popular U.S. television show in the 1950's called "The Lone Ranger." This lone lawman rode to rid the wild west of outlaws and was often vulnerable to attack. If we try to live our Christian lives alone, without the support of other believers, the devil can easily destroy us spiritually. We need each other. Hebrews 10:24-

REFLECTION
Why do we need to be connected to believers in the local church?
What does Hebrews 10:24-25 say we should spend time with other believers?

1. For the sake of hardening + Sharpening, + keeping both.

82. To spend more + more time w/ one another till Christ's comming for encouragement.

25 tells us, *And let us consider how we may spur one another on toward love and good deeds. Let us not give up meeting together, as some are in the habit of doing, but let us encourage one another— and all the more as you see the Day approaching.*

Jesus Christ is coming back soon. We need to stir one another up to be on fire for our Lord Jesus Christ. Meeting together regularly encourages each of us to hold firmly to Christ. God has a plan for us to assemble together on a regular basis so that we can receive teaching, encouragement and be equipped for the work of ministry. He calls this group of believers the "church." In this book, we will learn about the importance of being solidly connected to a local church.

The church—"called out ones"

What is the *church*, exactly? The church is not a building or a meeting or a program. The church of Jesus Christ is simply *people*. As believers, we are the church. The word *church* literally means *called out ones*. The church then, is a group of people who have been called out of spiritual darkness into the light of God's kingdom.

When we come to Christ, we are immediately a part of the universal church of Christ which includes every believer who has ever named the name of Christ from every nation of the world. Jesus talks about His universal church in Matthew 16:18. *And I tell you that you are Peter, and on this rock I will build my church, and the gates of Hades will not overcome it.* I have had the privilege of traveling to six continents of the world. Everywhere I go, I find believers from completely different backgrounds, different skin colors and different cultures who have one thing in common. They all have the same heavenly Father, have received Jesus Christ as Lord, and are part of the same family.

One time, while flying in an airplane, the businessman sitting next to me began to tell me about the corporation he represents. Then he asked me, "What do you do?" I told him that I am a part of the largest corporation in the world. "In fact," I said, "we are now in every country of the world." Of course, I was talking about the kingdom of God—God's wonderful and universal family, the church of Jesus Christ.

The Bible is talking about the universal church when it says that all the saints of the whole church of God, and all His children in heaven and earth will acknowledge that Jesus Christ is alone worthy...*with your blood you purchased men for God from every tribe and language and people and nation (Revelation 5:9).*

Jesus has promised that He will build His church and the gates of hell will not prevail against it (Matthew 16:18). We can be assured that regardless of what happens in the world today, Jesus Christ is building His church, and we have the privilege of being a part of it.

But the word *church* also refers to the *local* church. Within God's universal church family are *local* churches in each community which provide the support and love each believer needs.

REFLECTION
What is the church?
What is the universal church?
What is the local church?

1. The true bride & body of Christ
2. The entire body everywhere
3. love supporting community body.

A baby Christian needs a family

Every believer needs a "support system" to survive. When I have the privilege of leading someone to Christ, I often tell him that he is now a "baby Christian" and needs to understand four important truths of spiritual nourishment. First of all, every baby needs to eat and drink. That's why the Bible says in 1 Peter 2:2 that baby Christians need to first drink the milk of God's Word so they can begin to grow. *Like newborn babies, crave pure spiritual milk, so that by it you may grow up in your salvation.*

Secondly, to remain alive, every baby needs to breathe. Baby Christians (and mature ones!) breathe spiritually through prayer—through communicating with our Father in heaven. The Bible tells us to "pray continually" (1 Thessalonians 5:17).

Thirdly, we need to exercise—to share our faith with others. The scriptures tell us, "Let the redeemed of the Lord say so..." (Psalms 107:2 NKJ).

And fourthly, baby Christians need to stay warm. We stay warm through being committed to other believers in a local church and having regular fellowship with them. We are a part of a spiritual family—a family of the redeemed who are joined under one Father in Christ. *For this reason I kneel before the Father, from whom his whole family in heaven and on earth derives its name (Ephesians 3:14-15).*

In the local church, we are part of a spiritual family united under Christ. This spiritual family gives us a place to grow and learn from other believers how to live our Christian lives. We need this input from others.

You will find that there is no perfect local church. However, this is no excuse for not getting involved in a church in our communities. If we could find a church that was perfect, the moment we joined, the church would no longer be perfect, because we are not perfect!

Our salvation, of course, does not come through being joined to a local church; it comes by knowing God our Father through a personal relationship with Jesus Christ. When we join to Christ, we become his sons and daughters. *"I will be a Father to you, and you will be my sons and daughters," says the Lord Almighty (2 Corinthians 6:18).*

However, once we are children of God, we should want to join other Christians so we can receive their love and care. As soon as we are saved, we should ask the Lord where He desires to place us in His family in a church in our community.

REFLECTION
What are the four things a spiritual baby needs in order to grow spiritually?
What does our heavenly Father call us (2 Corinthians 6:18)?

1 spirit. food(milk) 2 prayer
3 testimony 4 commitment to a
body. 5. His children.

The local church is God's army

We need one another. We are not supposed to live the Christian life alone. The Lord has called us to be a company of spiritual soldiers who serve in His spiritual army. *Endure hardship with us like a good soldier of Christ Jesus (2 Timothy 2:3).*

A former military officer once told me that what kept him going in the war more than anything else was the camaraderie that he developed with fellow soldiers. We are in a spiritual war and we need the support of our fellow Christian soldiers because we are fighting the devil who is out to kill, steal and destroy the people of God (John 10:10).

Armies are made up of small groups called platoons. In the New Testament church, the believers met from house to house (in small groups) as well as in the temple (in large groups). Meeting in a local church fellowship is especially important because it allows us to be

DAY 4

encouraged and trained as spiritual soldiers. It is so important to find the place where God can use us best in His kingdom.

The local church is not only for training to go into the world. Just as all armies have medical units, the church is also a place we can be cared for, healed and strengthened when we are weak. It is a place where we can be set free to live transformed, victorious lives so we can go out to the spiritual battlefield with power. By the power and authority of Jesus Christ, in local churches, people can be set free from besetting sins, life-controlling problems and bad habits.

Sometimes today, churches look more like social clubs than a spiritual army. People attend meetings for the social interaction and forget their true purpose. God has called His church to return to its original purpose to be a standard of righteousness in our generation. Isaiah 59:19 (NKJ) says that *when the enemy comes in like a flood, the Spirit of the Lord will lift up a standard against him.* The church of Jesus Christ is a standard that the Lord is raising up against the enemy who wants to destroy this generation. Each of us needs to find our place in God's army, the local church, and do our part.

REFLECTION
Why must we be like soldiers? Who are we fighting (John 10:10)?

1. encouragement, training + bolstering, support.
2. A spiritual army

Fitting together

Like a building that is made up of blocks that have been placed on a wall with mortar, as the church, we are living stones built together through relationships with one another.

As you come to him, the living Stone—rejected by men but chosen by God and precious to him—you also, like living stones, are being built into a spiritual house to be a holy priesthood, offering spiritual sacrifices acceptable to God through Jesus Christ (1 Peter 2:4-5).

For we are God's fellow workers; you are God's field, God's building (1 Corinthians 3:9).

In these scriptures, notice that the Lord calls us a "building" and also a "field." Not only are we to be in relationship with other believers, we should know where we fit in our spiritual "field."

Many times when I fly over countries that have beautiful farm lands, I can see various crops growing in distinct fields. Each local church is a distinct field with believers planted there so they can

Biblical Foundations

grow and reproduce within that particular "field." The Lord's desire is for us to reproduce the life of Jesus in others. It all starts when we are committed to Jesus and to a local church where we can receive help to grow in Christ and help others to grow in the Lord.

That's why it is so important for the local church to be made up of small groups of believers who meet together. It is impossible for a believer to be touching (relating to) dozens or hundreds of people, but in smaller groups we can practically touch a few people. In some churches these may be called Sunday School classes or Bible study groups. Other churches may use the term home fellowships or cell groups or house churches.

Kelly, a young divorced mother of two, learned just how valuable the relationships she had with those in her small group were. She had let the insurance lapse on her car and then had an accident causing her driver's license to be suspended for three months. She wondered how she would care for her children because she would lose her job as a school bus driver. Her small group rallied around her in prayer and practical help. During her three months without a job, she had a ride whenever she needed one. Bags of groceries appeared at her doorstep. Kelly learned that God provides through the people she was "built together with."

Jesus had a small group of twelve disciples. Moses was commanded by the Lord to break the Israelites down into groups of tens (Exodus 18). We all have a need for relationships and to get to know others who can provide mutual support as we learn to grow in God and fulfill His purposes in our lives. This best happens in smaller groups with everyone working toward a common goal.

REFLECTION
How are you God's field and building (1 Corinthians 3:9)? Do you know where you fit into God's kingdom?

1. Our Function is to grow, reproduce + feed as a harvest.

2. Yes, + finding out more + more as I fellowship + grow.

The local church provides leadership and protection

Why, you may ask, is it so important to be involved in a local church? For one thing, the local church provides leaders to equip us in our Christian walk. The early church was encouraged to appoint elders in every city (local church). *The reason I left you in Crete was that you might straighten out what was left unfinished and appoint elders in every town, as I directed you (Titus 1:5).*

One of the Lord's purposes for the local church is to provide eldership or spiritual leadership who can equip us, encourage us and serve us as "undershepherds" under Jesus (who is the Chief Shepherd). These leaders have clear instructions what their role is. *And we urge you, brothers, warn those who are idle, encourage the timid,*

REFLECTION
What are some things spiritual leaders provide in the local church (1 Thessalonians 5:14-15)?

help the weak, be patient with everyone. Make sure that nobody pays back wrong for wrong, but always try to be kind to each other and to everyone else (1 Thessalonians 5:14-15).

This verse tells us that the Lord provides protection and discipline for His people through leaders in the local church. Leaders are to be people of love and patience as they encourage those they serve. They are there to give guidance and correction in love.

In Matthew 18:15-17, Jesus tells how the local church can provide discipline and restoration to a wayward member. *If your brother sins against you, go and show him his fault, just between the two of you. If he listens to you, you have won your brother over. But if he will not listen, take one or two others along, so that "every matter may be established by the testimony of two or three witnesses." If he refuses to listen to them, tell it to the church; and if he refuses to listen even to the church, treat him as you would a pagan or a tax collector.*

If a Christian believer sins against us, Jesus instructs us to confront him one-on-one. If he does not listen, we should go with "two or more" believers and again appeal to him to repent. If he still does not hear us, we should "tell it to the church." This is referring to the local church, because it would be impossible to take it to the

i. Counsel 2. encourager (cheer leader)
3. support 4. A patient parent figure.
5. teacher 6. A Friend.

universal church! The local church leaders will help to restore such a person back into fellowship.

Local church leaders have the responsibility to keep watch over us by protecting, directing, correcting and encouraging us. *Keep watch over yourselves and all the flock of which the Holy Spirit has made you overseers (Acts 20:28).*

Vulnerable without a local church

Sometimes, through disillusionment, disappointment or spiritual pride, believers find themselves uninvolved in a local church. This leaves them very vulnerable. The Bible tells us in 1 Corinthians 10:13, *No temptation has seized you except what is common to man. And God is faithful; he will not let you be tempted beyond what you can bear. But when you are tempted, he will also provide a way out so that you can stand up under it.*

The local church is often "the way out" the Lord has prepared for His people during an onslaught of the devil. When we fellowship with other believers, we realize that we are not alone in the temptations that we face. We receive spiritual protection, strength and oversight from the spiritual leaders the Lord has placed in our lives. The Lord's plan is to use the local church to protect us, help us grow, and equip us to be all that we can be in Jesus Christ.

D.L. Moody, an evangelist from the late 1800's, was used of the Lord to lead a million people to Christ. Many times when he preached, he had a choir that included singers from many churches in the community in which he was preaching. A lady came to him one day and said, "Mr. Moody, I would like to sing in your choir." When Moody asked her which local church she represented, she said, "I am involved in the universal church."

Moody said to her, "Then find the pastor of the universal church and sing in his choir." In other words, Moody was concerned about this lady's noninvolvement in a local church. He recognized the need to be committed to a local church for spiritual protection and accountability.

Spiritual leaders and other believers in the local church are there to exhort you, comfort you and uphold you in prayer!

REFLECTION
Why are we vulnerable without a local fellowship of believers to support us?

l- It opens us up for temptation + the buffering of the devil.

CHAPTER 2

Spiritual Family Relationships

KEY MEMORY VERSE
You also, like living stones, are being built into
a spiritual house to be a holy priesthood,
offering spiritual sacrifices acceptable to
God through Jesus Christ.
1 Peter 2:5

The church is made up of family relationships

Many young couples who get married are in for a big surprise. They thought they were only marrying one person, but they realize after the wedding they married into an entire family! They have to get to know grandparents, uncles and aunts, cousins, dad and mom and all the rest of the in-laws. In the family of God, when you and I make a decision to become a part of a local church, we become a part of an entire church family. Galatians 3:26 tells us that sonship with God involves brotherhood with Jesus. Christians are related as family. We are all brothers (and sisters) through Jesus. *You are all sons of God through faith in Christ Jesus.*

In the Old Testament, God's people were always described as part of a larger family. The children of Israel were involved in one of twelve tribes. Each tribe was made up of a group of clans, and each clan was made up of a group of families. Gideon mentions his family, clan and tribe in Judges 6:15. *My clan is the weakest in Manasseh [tribe], and I am the least in my family.* Even today, the Lord continues to see each of us as a part of various spiritual spheres or families.

First, I believe the Lord sees me as an individual believer bought by the blood of Jesus.

He also recognizes that I am a part of a spiritual church family. For me, that spiritual family starts with the small group of believers I meet with weekly. In small groups, we are nurtured, equipped to serve and given the opportunity to reach out. Most churches have small groups of believers who meet together—Sunday School classes, youth groups, Bible studies, or in fellowships of believers who meet in homes. This kind of small group fellowship is one aspect of a spiritual family.

REFLECTION
Describe the way your local group of believers is related to other groups. Do you feel like a part of the church family?

cell, church body, sister churches, network.
Yes.

Another aspect of spiritual family life happens when whole clusters of small groups relate closely together to form a *congregation* of believers. When I meet on a Sunday morning with my local church congregation, my small group and many others come together to worship and receive the Word of God together. This is an extended spiritual family. According to Romans 16, the believers in Rome met together in homes. It also is clear they were in relationship with one another throughout the city in extended spiritual family relationships or congregations.

A third sphere of spiritual family relationships often refers to a church denomination or *family of churches*. Whenever a group of churches work together as a "network of churches" or an "apostolic fellowship" they form a larger sphere of family relationships. Our church is a part of a family of churches which partner together from various parts of the world, representing a larger spiritual family.

The Israelites were made up of twelve tribes and a multitude of clans and families. They were corporately known as "the children of Israel." In the same way, the church of Jesus Christ is made up of believers in small groups, congregations and denominations who together represent the kingdom of God.

Family relationships bring unity

No matter what our church affiliation or denomination, we become one family through Christ. When we realize that the walls have been broken down and we need each other as fellow believers in Christ, we will know for sure that every church group in the body of Christ is important to Him. *There is neither Jew nor Greek, slave nor free, male nor female, for you are all one in Christ Jesus (Galatians 3:28).*

Every church in every community and every denomination or family of churches has certain strengths to contribute to help the greater body of Christ. God uses many different church families to accomplish His purposes here on earth. We are called by the Lord to link arms with other churches, denominations and groups of believers so we can with one voice glorify our God and work together to build His kingdom.

Throughout history, there have been many times when, by His Holy Spirit, God would raise up various "movements," new families of churches and denominations to bring reform or refreshment to the church. For example, many Methodist churches are traced back to the 18th and 19th centuries when John Wesley and the team of men who worked closely with him obeyed the call from the Lord to share the gospel of Jesus Christ and to "plant" new groups of believers in the nations of the world. Today you can find Methodist church buildings all over the world.

The town I live in has a Moravian church. The Moravians, who have their roots in Europe, were sent to many nations of the world to share the gospel. In fact, they prayed around the clock 24 hours a day for 100 years, as they sent missionaries to the nations of the world to share the gospel of Jesus Christ and start new churches. They had a real sense of *family* as they labored together.

REFLECTION
Why is it important to recognize we need each other in the body of Christ?
Why do local churches need to be in relationship with other churches?

Throughout the 1960's and 70's, the Charismatic movement literally exploded throughout the world. God was telling His church that every believer needs to be filled with the Holy Spirit and experience the gifts of the Holy Spirit. God continues to move among His people who are citizens of His kingdom. We are linked together in unity by our family relationships!

New wineskins bring new life

DAY 3

I believe the Lord wants to pour out His Spirit in our generation. As He does, thousands of people will come into the kingdom of God. Jesus tells us to open our eyes and realize there are many lost in the world who need to be saved. *I tell you, open your eyes and look at the fields! They are ripe for harvest (John 4:35).*

But how can these new believers be "harvested?" Traditional, modern-day church structures and programs cannot accommodate a huge harvest. They already have their hands full. I believe we constantly need new churches starting up to provide new wineskins or structures for new believers in Jesus Christ. *Neither do men pour new wine into old wineskins. If they do, the skins will burst, the wine will run out and the wineskins will be ruined. No, they pour new wine into new wineskins, and both are preserved (Matthew 9:17).*

A new wineskin is like a balloon—flexible and pliable. Putting a new Christian (new wine) into an old church structure can cause the structure to break, and the new Christian may be lost. New Christians should be placed in new church structures that are flexible and able to encourage their spiritual growth. Such new

#1 Each one of us, unique & talented differently to perform different functions & serve as different parts of the body of Christ to comprise the whole body were 1st important to God, which should be important to us.

20 *Biblical Foundations*

Because we are linked in unity & agreement in relationship

"wineskins" may be a small group of believers meeting in a house church or cell group. In small groups, people can be easily nurtured, discipled, and trained as leaders.

I believe the Lord will be raising up many new wineskins to help bring in the harvest. God is preparing laborers to reach the masses with the gospel of Jesus Christ in our generation. He will require many of us to be involved with new groups of believers (new wineskins) in the future as the Lord calls us to the nations of the world. The newer house church networks (see Day 6) and cell groups will work with the more traditional churches already in our neighborhoods today.

We must work together. Sometimes people involved in newer churches have a tendency to look down on churches that have been around awhile. Instead, they should honor their "fathers"—those who have gone before them. And those in older churches should be glad when new movements and churches are started because they help to bring the gospel of Christ to a dying world.

We need every church body to be involved in planting new churches throughout the nations of the world. Every local church should have a vision that is much larger than themselves. Jesus instructed His disciples before He ascended into heaven. *But you will receive power when the Holy Spirit comes on you; and you will be my witnesses in Jerusalem, and in all Judea and Samaria, and to the ends of the earth (Acts 1:8).*

REFLECTION
Who are those "ripe for harvest" (John 4:35)?
Why are new wineskins important to new Christians?

In other words, the Lord is calling us as His church to share the gospel, make disciples and start new churches in our home town (Jerusalem), our region (Judea), our neighboring state or country (Samaria) and to the end of the earth (the nations of the world)!

Meeting house to house as a family

The early church understood the need for new churches to meet the needs of all the souls coming to the Lord. They met from house to house in small groups and also together in the temple, to receive teaching from the Word of God and worship the Lord together. *Every day they continued to meet together in the temple courts. They*

↳ The lost
↳ To be nurtured, trained, discipled as leaders
↳ loved the way "they" need loved and receive it.

broke bread in their homes and ate together with glad and sincere hearts, praising God and enjoying the favor of all the people. And the Lord added to their number daily those who were being saved (Acts 2:46-47).

After I gave my life to Jesus Christ in 1968, I had a tremendous hunger for God and for His Word. I started meeting with other young believers who were a part of a local church in our community to study the Bible and pray. One day we realized that God had called us to reach the lost around us, yet we were just sitting around enjoying a Bible study. We needed to become fishers of men (Mark 1:17).

During the next few years, my fiance and I helped start a youth ministry with a small band of young people who began to reach out to the unchurched youth of our community in Lancaster County, Pennsylvania, USA. We played sports and conducted various activities throughout the week for spiritually needy youngsters and teenagers. This kind of "friendship evangelism" produced results, and during the next few years, dozens of young people came to faith in Christ.

Those of us who served in this youth ministry were from various churches, so we also attempted to help the new believers find their place in our local congregations. Although the Christians in the local churches were friendly and helpful, something still wasn't "clicking." These young believers from unchurched backgrounds were just not being incorporated into the life of the established churches in our communities. We began to realize that there needed to be "new wineskins" for the "new wine."

The Lord clearly spoke to me about starting a new wineskin (new church structure of small groups) for the new wine (new Christians). After receiving the affirmation and blessing of the leadership of the church who had sent us out to start this new work, we stepped out in faith to start a new church in October, 1980. Since that time we've had the privilege of seeing people come to Christ and being built together in local churches throughout various nations of the world.

The church is people who are built together in a relationship with God and with one another who have been called by God with a common purpose and vision. They serve one another, reach out to those who need Christ, and support the local leadership that God raises up among them.

Real church is much more than going to a meeting every Sunday morning. For example, although we may not think about it often, a healthy tree needs to have a strong root system. In the same way, we have found in the church that what happens "underground" in cell groups (small groups where relationships are built) is of vital importance. When relationships are healthy and strong in small groups meeting together from house to house, the other church meetings will also be filled with life.

REFLECTION
How did the early church come together (Acts 2:46-47)? What happens when people are built together in relationship?

+ In temples, houses, over dinner (sm. Fellowship groups - cell groups & functions.)
+ serve one another, reach out to the lost, + support local leadership.

Families are connected

Can you imagine a builder taking a thousand bricks, throwing them on a big pile and calling that a building? Ridiculous! In order to build a building, a master planner needs to take hundreds and thousands of bricks and strategically place one upon another and then mortar them together. The mortar that God uses to build His kingdom is the mortar of relationships. God, the master planner, takes you and me and places us in His body in strategic places with others so we can fulfill the Lord's purposes.

Many times we call a building on the street corner the "church," but in reality the true church is "people." Praise God for buildings that we can use to worship Him and to be taught the Word of God; however, let's never confuse the church building for the true church, the people of God.

The Bible calls us "living stones." Each believer has been made alive through faith in our Lord Jesus Christ. The Lord builds us together with other Christians into a type of spiritual house or community. *You also, like living stones, are being built into a spiritual house to be a holy priesthood, offering spiritual sacrifices acceptable to God through Jesus Christ (1 Peter 2:5).*

We said before that the term "church" simply means "called-out ones"—those who are called out from the world's system to be a part of God's kingdom. To be a believer in Jesus Christ is to live counterculture to the world's system of selfishness. We live a new life in a new way, obeying the Word of God.

Jesus Christ lives in His church, which means He lives in His people, His called-out ones. Jesus dwells inside us as His people, His body. *From him the whole body, joined and held together by every supporting ligament, grows and builds itself up in love, as each part does its work (Ephesians 4:16).*

Like a human body, our shoulders and arms are linked together by joints and ligaments. These joints and ligaments, spiritually speaking, are relationships in the body of Christ. Believers joining together in a relationship who realize that Jesus Christ lives in them can supply one another with spiritual strength and life. That's why we need to be connected with other brothers and sisters in the body of Christ. I need my brothers and sisters to supply what I need to grow spiritually.

REFLECTION
From what is the church called out?
How are we connected as a family?

 # Sin & the worldly way,

 # In Christ, in relationship, in love for one another ie. they'll know we are his disciples by our love.

Where has God placed you?

The Lord who has created our bodies tells us that we are like a spiritual body. Aren't you grateful that your hand is attached to your arm? If your hand was attached to your ear, it would cause a lot of problems for your body! We need to be placed properly in the body of Christ so we can be effective.

1 Corinthians 12:18 tells us God arranges us just where He wants us to be. *But in fact God has arranged the parts in the body, every one of them, just as he wanted them to be.* It is important that we know where God has placed us in His church so that we can serve effectively. You see, it is not the church of *our* choice, but it is the church of *His* choice.

There are different sizes and shapes of churches in our communities in which we can get involved. What I call a "community church" is a traditional church, meeting in a building on a Sunday and reaching the local populace in the surrounding community. It is often about 50-500 in size. A "mega-church" also meets in a church building on a Sunday but it reaches a much broader geographical area. It is often well over 1,000 in size. Finally, what I call a "house church network" is a group of individual house churches, often meeting in homes, which are complete little churches led by their own elders. Each house church or "micro-church," meeting together at least once each week, works with other house churches and other types of churches in their area.

Where is God placing you in the body of Christ? There are many wonderful churches throughout the world today. The issue is not which church is best. Every church family has strengths and weaknesses. The issue is this: where has God called you to be placed in His church? Which group of believers has the Lord called you to labor with during this season of your life?

REFLECTION
Why does God want us in a particular place in His church (1 Corinthians 12:18)? What other options, beside the more traditional community church or mega-church, are there for you to experience "church"?

The Lord wants you to grow spiritually and use you to reach other people for Christ. Find a church family you can relate to and then get involved in reaching out to people. Perhaps the Lord wants to use your home as a place where a small group of believers can meet and grow spiritually. Open up your home! You can reproduce yourself spiritually by mentoring or discipling others to grow in their Christian lives. Find your niche in the body of Christ!

Families will multiply

We read in the book of Acts that the early church grew and multiplied. The Lord had given them His Holy Spirit and a clear strategy from His Word for the church to grow. These early believers remembered the words of our Lord Jesus before He went back to His Father in heaven. He told them to "go and make disciples of all the nations..." (Matthew 28:19). A few weeks later as they met from house to house throughout the city of Jerusalem, believers realized that they were responsible to help other new believers grow in their relationship with God.

This is called the principle of multiplication. Believers in small groups are taught and trained to grow in the Lord, and many will eventually be trained to lead their own small groups. This causes the church to rapidly multiply! The believers in each new group

for effectiveness

cell group, house church, network church, micro church.

continue to supply what the other believers need in order to grow spiritually, according to Ephesians 4:16.

In order for the local church and the home cell groups to stay healthy, they need to get a vision from God to grow in numbers and then to multiply to start other groups. The early church rapidly increased.

In those days when the number of disciples was increasing...the word of God spread. The number of disciples in Jerusalem increased rapidly...(Acts 6:1,7).

The church of Jesus Christ was multiplied. Every group of believers meeting in a small group needs to have a vision to multiply and start other cell groups or house churches. In this way the church will continue to be healthy and strong. People in a church or a cell group that do not reach out to bring people to Christ often stagnate and eventually die spiritually.

Our bodies are made up of cells. Cells in our body go through a process called mitosis. The process of mitosis is simply this: one cell divides and becomes two. Those two cells then in turn divide and become four. In our bodies, a cell that will not produce will eventually die. The same principle applies to the church of

REFLECTION
Explain the principle of multiplication.
What had to be spread before the church could multiply in Acts 6:1,7?

Jesus Christ. Believers in cell groups and house churches are called by God to have a vision to reach out to new people and see them saved and become a part of the body of Christ. As they grow, people are being multiplied through "spiritual mitosis."

God has called each of us and every local church to pray, to evangelize, and to make disciples. Let's expect the Lord to use us as He multiplies His life through us to others.

* Believers in a sm. group being trained by a leader to become leaders to start of lead sm, groups of believers to be trained by a leader...

\# Word of Gods

CHAPTER 3

Who is Watching Out for You?

KEY MEMORY VERSE

Now we ask you, brothers, to respect those who work hard among you, who are over you in the Lord and who admonish you. Hold them in the highest regard in love because of their work. Live in peace with each other.
1 Thessalonians 5:12-13

The importance of commitment to other believers

The early Christians had a very effective way of looking out for each other. They met from house to house in small groups so they could "practice loving each other." *Practice loving each other, for love comes from God and those who are loving and kind show that they are children of God, and they are getting to know him better (1 John 4:7 TLB).*

Love does not just happen. It must be practiced. It is not just a feeling of goodwill but a decision that motivates us to help people and meet their needs. We cannot practically be committed to love and care for hundreds or thousands of other people. Although we can worship and learn from the Word of God together in a large group, we can only be practically committed to a small group of people at a time. Paul ministered in large public meetings as well as small house groups, according to Acts 20:20. *I...have taught you publicly and from house to house.*

Practical Christianity happens when believers meet together to reach their neighbors and co-workers with the gospel of Jesus Christ and help each other grow spiritually mature in Christ. Believers in my church family regularly meet in small cell groups where we pray for those who are sick and hurting as we extend God's love and forgiveness to each other. Our commitment to each other is heartfelt and real. We really do look out for each other. Our home cell group is our spiritual family.

In some churches, believers show their commitment to other believers in their home cell group or house church by making a simple pledge to commit to them as their local church family. Making this commitment is not so much a doctrine or a philosophy but a commitment to Jesus and His people to look out for each other. I believe that a commitment to the local church is a commitment to God, His Word and other believers more than it is commitment to an institution or an organization. We really show our commitment to other believers in our small group by faithfully interacting and

> **REFLECTION**
> *How is a small home group a great way to promote true fellowship? How have you helped to meet the needs of others in your small group?*

It helps us learn by practice the benefits of fellowship & exercise our giftings one of which is hospitality.

Iron sharpening iron

Biblical Foundations

building relationships with them. They will know we care if we make them a priority in our lives.

Although the elders of our church are the ones who watch out for our spiritual welfare (as we will see in the next section), I am very grateful for the believers in my small group who practically serve me, pray for me and encourage me in my walk with Jesus Christ.

Leaders give us spiritual protection

According to Hebrews 13:7,17, God places spiritual leaders in our lives who are accountable to God to watch out for us. *Remember your leaders, who spoke the word of God to you. Consider the outcome of their way of life and imitate their faith.*

Obey your leaders and submit to their authority. They keep watch over you as men who must give an account. Obey them so that their work will be a joy, not a burden, for that would be of no advantage to you.

Spiritual leaders in our lives give us spiritual protection, and we need to follow their example as they place their faith in Jesus Christ. We should remember them, receive the Word of God from them, obey them, be submissive to them, and do all that we can so their responsibility is joyful and not grievous. The Bible tells us that the devil is like a roaring lion seeking to devour us (1 Peter 5:8). That's why we need church leaders—to protect us and encourage us.

According to 1 Thessalonians 5:12-13, the Lord has called us to recognize and honor those He has placed in our lives as spiritual leaders. *Now we ask you, brothers, to respect those who work hard among you, who are over you in the Lord and who admonish you. Hold them in the highest regard in love because of their work. Live in peace with each other.*

I have spent much of my time traveling to various nations of the world in the past years, and I have been blessed over and over again by the spiritual leaders that the Lord has placed in my life. Our small group leaders, local pastors and elders have provided a tremendous sense of encouragement and protection to me and my family. Many times these precious brothers and sisters in Christ have prayed, encouraged and exhorted us. These spiritual leaders have encour-

REFLECTION
List ways your spiritual leaders have watched out for you.

† Bob has been my mentor my counceler my friend, my pastor, my spiritual Father, salt + life + light that examples Christ for me in my life.

aged me and held me accountable to take enough time with my family even though my travel schedule can be hectic. I am grateful to God that my spiritual leaders have my best interests at heart.

Leaders help keep us on track

The Bible tells us in Acts 2:42 that the early believers "continued steadfastly in the apostles' doctrine and fellowship, in the breaking of bread, and in prayers." The early believers continued to study the scriptures and learn from the preaching and teaching of the early church leaders. Paul, the apostle, told the Ephesian elders in Acts 20:28-31 that the enemy will try to bring heresy into the church of Jesus Christ. *Keep watch over yourselves and all the flock of which the Holy Spirit has made you overseers. Be shepherds of the church of God, which he bought with his own blood. I know that after I leave, savage wolves will come in among you and will not spare the flock. Even from your own number men will arise and distort the truth in order to draw away disciples after them. So be on your guard! Remember that for three years I never stopped warning each of you night and day with tears.*

The Lord has given us His Word and places spiritual leaders in our lives to keep us from heresy (wrong teaching that is spiritually destructive). There are many "voices" today vying for our attention. We can trust the Word of God and we can trust spiritual leaders who have good "fruit" (character and integrity) in their lives (Matthew 7:15-20).

REFLECTION
Why is heresy so devastating to a church? How do we keep from heresy, according to Acts 2:42?

I am grateful for the spiritual leaders God has raised up worldwide. There is no one church or family of churches (denomination) who has all of the truth. We need to study the Word of God and learn from spiritual leaders, not only in our local church, but in the greater body of Christ. Spiritual leaders help us to keep from becoming sidetracked by minor issues (Romans 14:5) and heresies that would try to come into the body of Christ.

It misleads the church even raises up false teachers that are believable and (angel of dark appearring as - angel of light) whose soul purpose is to steer you into harms way & away from truth.

look for fruit, check scripture seek good counsel, look at character & integrity

Biblical Foundations

Leaders equip

DAY 4

God calls believers with spiritual leadership abilities to build up and strengthen the believers in the church so that all believers can fulfill their work of service. God releases specific leadership gifts in the body of Christ so the people with those gifts can equip us for service according to Ephesians 4:11-12. *It was he who gave some to be apostles, some to be prophets, some to be evangelists, and some to be pastors and teachers, to prepare God's people for works of service, so that the body of Christ may be built up.*

These five ministry gifts (apostle, prophet, evangelist, pastor, teacher) are given to various individuals in the body of Christ who are then responsible to train and equip others. The gifts are "deposited" in spiritual leaders who are called by the Lord to train us to minister to others effectively. Those who have these gifts are able to train each believer for a lifetime of ministry.

Apostles are given to the church to help us receive a vision from the Lord to reach the world. Prophets are given to train us to listen to the voice of God. Evangelists are called of God to train us and to "stir us up'" to reach the lost. Pastors are commissioned by the Lord to encourage us, protect us, and show us how to make disciples. Teachers have a divine anointing to assist us in understanding the Word of God. Some spiritual leaders may have more than one gift in operation in their lives.

God's plan is to use these five gifts in His local church as much as possible to equip us (the saints) for the work of ministry. When we are equipped, we will be able to minister, too! Every believer is a minister. A pastor or church leader is not the only one who can minister. Every believer is called to minister to others in Jesus' name. You can receive input from someone with a spiritual leadership ability (gift) and be equipped and strengthened as you come to maturity as a Christian.

REFLECTION
Name the five ministry gifts given to the body of Christ. Have you been equipped and released in a particular gift so that you can minister to others?

Leaders lead

DAY 5

What can we learn from the New Testament about how leadership works practically in a local church? Acts 15 tells about a dispute in the church and how they solved it. Paul, sent out as an apostle, met

✝ Apostles, pastors, prophets, evangelists, teachers.

✝ work in progress.

with the leadership of the church in Jerusalem to discuss a problem. James was the clear leader of the Jerusalem church along with a team of elders who worked with him. *The next day Paul and the rest of us went to see James, and all the elders were present (Acts 21:18).*

James and his team of elders were responsible to work out solutions to problems as they prayed and heard from the Father. At every local church, there should be a team of elders, along with one person who is called to give clear oversight to this team and the local church. In fact, this principle applies in every area of the church. God calls teams of people to work together for a common goal; however, someone always has been chosen by the Lord to be the leader of this team. *May the Lord, the God of the spirits of all mankind, appoint a man over this community (Numbers 27:16).*

Every local church, every family of churches and every cell group or house church needs to have a clear leadership team, along with someone who has been chosen of God to give leadership to the team. For example, in a husband-wife relationship, there is a real sense of teamwork. In a healthy marriage, the husband and wife make decisions together; however the husband is called to be the head of the home and should love and care for his wife. When, in times of crisis, a decision has to be made, the husband is responsible for the final decision.

When an airplane is flying, everyone works together as a team. However, during times of crisis, take off, and landing, who is in charge? The pilot. This is based on a spiritual truth. For instance, in your local church, God has called someone to give clear leadership to the church, yet at the same time, there should be a real sense of teamwork among the leadership team.

Acts 14:21-23 tells us that Paul and Barnabas were concerned that every local church in every area had clear eldership (spiritual leadership) appointed among them. In the New Testament, we see various types of spiritual leadership mentioned. Acts 15:6 says, *The apostles and elders met to consider this question.* The elders were those who gave oversight to the local congregations. The apostles were those who had a larger sphere of oversight because they were called to oversee church leaders from various parts of the world. As "apostolic overseers," they were responsible to care for, oversee, encourage and equip local elders who served the people in their local area or sphere of influence. *We, however, will not boast beyond measure, but within the limits of the sphere which God appointed us—a sphere which especially includes you (2 Corinthians 10:13 NKJ).*

Paul, the apostle, told the Corinthian believers that they were within his sphere of responsibility. Paul was not a local elder in the Corinthian church; however, he was responsible to give oversight to the eldership who oversaw the work of God in that area. Paul called himself an apostle. Various denominations use different terminology when referring to these apostolic overseers in today's church; however, they still fulfill a similar role of overseeing pastors and elders in the local church.

REFLECTION
According to Acts 15, how did the early church model the fact that team leadership is more effective than one single person leading alone? Why is it important to have clear leadership for a team?

Leaders chosen by God and confirmed by His people

Since it is the Lord's plan for His church to grow and multiply, He is constantly desiring to release new leaders in His church. The leadership at the church of Antioch came together to fast and pray, and then the Holy Spirit called Barnabas and Saul to a new work of planting churches. *In the church at Antioch there were prophets and teachers...While they were worshiping the Lord and fasting, the Holy Spirit said, "Set apart for me Barnabas and Saul for the work to which I have called them." So after they had fasted and prayed, they placed their hands on them and sent them off (Acts 13:1-4).*

Barnabas and Saul were sent out to do God's work by the Holy Spirit. The Holy Spirit is the One who calls church leaders and believers into areas of ministry. After they were called, the spiritual leaders at Antioch affirmed the new leaders, laid their hands on them, and prayed for them to be sent away to fulfill the Lord's call on their lives.

In today's church, different church families have various ways of choosing leadership. Some churches are governed by a democracy. A democracy is basically a church ruled by the people. Either a committee is formed or there is a type of consensus or vote to make decisions about church leadership.

✱ They had leaders over the congregation to equip & oversee the church
+ leaders to oversee leaders to make sure they
were doing so responsibly. ✱ To ensure what is being preached truely is the gospel + not tradition

What is the Church? 33

Others are governed by a theocracy. I am of the persuasion that God is restoring theocracy to His church. Church government by theocracy means the leadership of the church fast and pray, and the Holy Spirit speaks to them about whom He is calling to spiritual leadership. God's people then, through fasting and prayer, give their affirmation to the Holy Spirit calling this person to spiritual leadership. In the New Testament, spiritual leaders were called by God this way.

It is my understanding that leadership in a local church (or in a cell group) should be appointed because *God* is the One who has called this spiritual leader into an area of oversight and spiritual service. When God calls a person to leadership, he will be confirmed by other leaders and the body of Christ around him. Remember David the shepherd boy who was called to be the king of Israel? The Lord called David as a young boy. He was anointed with oil through Samuel the prophet (1 Samuel 16:13); however, it was many years later until David

REFLECTION
What does church government by theocracy mean?

was affirmed by others to be the new king of Israel. Between the time of his call and the time of the fulfillment of this prophecy, David experienced many dark hours hiding out from a demonized king who was trying to kill him. But the day came when David was confirmed to be the king of Israel by other leaders around him and then eventually by the people of God.

I believe it is also advantageous to have spiritual leaders from outside the local congregation also involved in this process of discernment regarding leadership. In Titus 1:5, Paul tells Titus to be responsible for the process of choosing leadership in the churches in Crete. *The reason I left you in Crete was that you might straighten out what was left unfinished and appoint elders in every town, as I directed you.* Anyone who has been given authority by the Lord needs to also be under authority. Titus was serving under Paul's leadership as an apostle in the early church.

✝ Elders seeking God's face + God's choice of divine appointment to leadership for us.

Leaders are always servants

Leaders in the body of Christ are called to be servants. Jesus Christ was the greatest leader who ever lived, and He said, ...*whoever wants to become great among you must be your servant, and whoever wants to be first must be your slave—just as the Son of Man did not come to be served, but to serve, and to give his life as a ransom for many (Matthew 20:26b-28).*

If someone comes to me and says he feels called to be a leader, I am not impressed with how much charisma he has or with his knowledge of the Bible. The real key to his ability to lead depends on whether or not he loves Jesus, loves His people and is willing to serve.

Churches often acknowledge individuals within their congregation who have a special ministry in serving as "deacons." The Bible tells us that deacons were first to be tested before they were set apart as deacons (1 Timothy 3:10). When someone desires to be involved in any type of church leadership, there should first be a period of time for him to be tested. Does he really have the heart of a servant? This is not implying that there is something wrong with him; it simply means that he needs to have time to see how he fits in with the other believers in the local church.

People are like pieces to a puzzle. Some people fit together and others do not. That's the way it is in the kingdom of God. It takes time until we know whether or not God has placed people together so they can work smoothly and effectively with one another.

Sometimes there are problems in churches which have occurred because the pastor or leader was brought in with good intentions, but the pieces just didn't seem to fit. If my arm is broken, a doctor would set it with a cast. It would take some time for it to be bonded back together. People need time to be bonded together. As the Lord calls you to be involved in a local church, allow the Lord to take enough time for you to be knit together in relationships

REFLECTION
How was Jesus the model for servant-leadership?
Why must leaders be tested before leadership responsibility is given to them?

To show the approved of God.

with those in the church. It takes time for these relationships to be built. Relationships are built on trust, and trust takes time. These relationships can be built effectively with a small group of believers.

He left power + glory + clothed Himself with the Flesh suit of creation to lead, teach, + care for us up close + personal to die in humility as a curse at His own creations hands(as) willingly then as He died He plead our case + asked our forgiveness from the Father.

What is the Church?

35

Consequently, when someone comes into a local church and becomes a part of a small group, wise spiritual leaders will give God the time He needs to work in the life of this believer before placing him into spiritual leadership. As the grace of God is evident in this believer's life, it will not be long until people around him will begin to look to him for leadership. Spiritual leaders who are sensitive to the Holy Spirit will begin to release him into areas of leadership, perhaps as an assistant leader in the small group. This can be a training ground for future leadership.

CHAPTER 4

Our Commitment to the Local Church

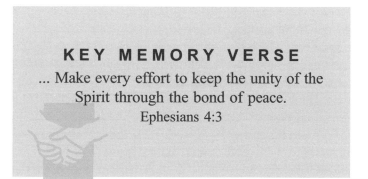

KEY MEMORY VERSE
... Make every effort to keep the unity of the
Spirit through the bond of peace.
Ephesians 4:3

Common vision in the church

Did you ever go to a church meeting and feel like it was a really nice group of believers, but somehow you just didn't fit in? Although there was nothing wrong with this church, God simply wasn't calling you there. Every believer needs to be placed within the body of Christ so that he will be working hand-in-hand with believers with whom he shares a common vision. At the same time, we need to confirm the rest of the body of Christ around us so that God's purposes can be fulfilled. Remember, God is a creative God. In the same way the Lord created you and me, He created various kinds of congregations in His church family. Together they fulfill the purposes of God.

The scripture says that we should not plow with a donkey and an ox together (Deuteronomy 22:10). Why? Because they move at different paces. We need to be sure that the people we are "walking with" in our local church are those with whom the Lord has placed us, so that we can walk in unity, and He can command a blessing.

How good and pleasant it is when brothers live together in unity!

...For there the Lord bestows his blessing, even life forevermore (Psalms 133:1,3b).

You can make hamburgers at McDonald's, but if you go to work at another restaurant, they will make hamburgers a bit differently from the way you were trained to do it. Every church has a different way of doing things. They have different visions the Lord has given them to fulfill.

For example, some churches prefer singing hymns with an organ while others prefer choruses and worship with a band. Some churches may focus more on systematic Bible teaching, while others are more focused on evange-lism. We need to be a part of a church where we can agree with the basic "values" the spiritual leaders are teaching us.

REFLECTION
How does your personal vision compare with your church's (or small group's)

In a cell-based church or house church, everyone is a part of a small group where they can be accountable to their brothers and sisters in the way they live their Christian lives. These smaller groups have a vision to nurture believers and help them with "blind spots" in their lives.

✱ Very similar, yet some importances may vary and we may not see eye to eye on.

Biblical Foundations

A church's vision encourages us to support and submit to the leadership that God raises up among us. When a church body agrees to a common vision, it will be easier to "live together in unity!"

Know where you are called

Maybe you are saying, "How do I really know where God has placed me in His church?" First of all, you need to pray. Ask God, "Who are the Christian believers with whom I have a relationship?" Remember, the Lord places His people in relationships so they can serve Him. The scripture also tells us we must *let the peace of Christ rule in our hearts (Colossians 3:15).* In other words, you will know as you pray and take steps of faith and obedience.

We are living in the last days, and God tells us He is going to pour out His Spirit on all flesh. You can expect it to happen. The Bible says in Acts 2:17-18, *"In the last days," God says, "I will pour out my Spirit on all people. Your sons and daughters will prophesy, your young men will see visions, your old men will dream dreams. Even on my servants, both men and women, I will pour out my Spirit in those days, and they will prophesy."*

When the Lord poured out His Spirit in Acts, chapter 2, the church was birthed in Jerusalem. Believers met from house to house all over the city. As God pours out His Spirit in our generation, there will be a need for many new "wineskins." New churches will be raised up to take care of the coming harvest as new believers are birthed into the kingdom of God. Some may be community churches, others mega-churches and still others house churches or "micro-churches." God may call you to be part of a new fellowship of believers in the future.

Trust God to lead you to spiritual leaders who are open and transparent with their own lives. Spiritual leaders need to be transparent with their Christian lives, sharing their weaknesses as well as their strengths.

Ask the Lord to lead you to be-lievers who will be willing to pray with you to help you discern where the Lord is placing you in His body. God wants you connected to a local church where you can be trained, pro-tected and available to serve others.

REFLECTION

According to Colossians 3:15, what is the basic evidence that you are where God wants you to be?

✱ The peace of Christ ruling in my heart despite circumstance or comfort.

Agreement in the local church

All believers in a local church should know what their church believes. Every local church should also have a clear "statement of faith" and a written statement of the specific vision the Lord has given them to fulfill. Billy Graham and a group of spiritual leaders met in Lausanne, Switzerland, in 1974 and the Lord gave them a statement of faith called the *Lausanne Covenant*. This is the covenant that our church, along with thousands of other churches throughout the world, has used as a statement of faith. This statement of faith declares that there is one God and that the Bible is the inspired Word of God. It states all of the major doctrines that are so precious to us as true believers in Jesus Christ.[1] If you are considering joining a church family, ask for their statement of faith.

Besides knowing and agreeing with your church's statement of faith, it is God's will for church leadership and all of God's people to work together in unity. *Make every effort to keep the unity of the Spirit through the bond of peace (Ephesians 4:3).*

As we preserve the unity in our local church family, God will continue to pour out His blessing on us. If someone comes to you regarding a problem with leadership in your local church, tell him that he needs to talk to the person with whom he has the problem. There is no place for gossip or slander in the kingdom of God. The enemy will use it as a wedge of disunity. If believers in your small group do not agree with the leadership of the local church, they need to pray and then discuss their problem with the leadership, not with other believers in the church. Those in leadership should be open to listening to the concerns of those they lead. Godly leaders will want to hear your appeals. The enemy knows that a breakdown of unity will hinder the work of God more than any other thing in the local church. That's why the scripture says in 1 Corinthians 1:10 that we should appeal to each other. *I appeal to you, brothers, in the name of our Lord Jesus Christ, that all of you agree with one another so that there may be no divisions among you and that you may be perfectly united in mind and thought.*

REFLECTION
What is your responsibility in keeping unity in your small group, your church, your family? Why is it so important for believers in a local church to agree (1 Corinthians 1:10)?

[1] A copy of the Lausanne Covenant appears at www.dcfi.org.

40   *Biblical Foundations*

Support your church's vision

If every person called to be a part of a local church is committed to a relationship with a small group of believers within the church, there will be healthy relationships throughout the church. In the New Testament, God's people met as small groups of believers in homes. Everyone was needed. *Now the body is not made up of one part but of many. If the foot should say, "Because I am not a hand, I do not belong to the body," it would not for that reason cease to be part of the body. And if the ear should say, "Because I am not an eye, I do not belong to the body," it would not for that reason cease to be part of the body. If the whole body were an eye, where would the sense of hearing be? If the whole body were an ear, where would the sense of smell be? But in fact God has arranged the parts in the body, every one of them, just as he wanted them to be (1 Corinthians 12:14-18).*

Just as every member of the human body is important, every member of the local church should know where and how he is connected to the body of our Lord Jesus Christ. If you have questions about the specific vision of your local church, it is important that you sit down with church leadership to gain a clear understanding of what the Lord has called your church to do. It is of utmost importance that believers support the vision and the leadership of the local church in which they serve. If you cannot support the leadership and the vision of your local church, then the Lord may be calling you into another local church.

Did you ever notice how a group of houses in a community may all look the same on the outside because they were built by a builder with one particular style? Most of these houses, however, are different inside. In the same way, although they may "look" similar, various churches have different callings from the Lord, and as a spiritual family, have their own uniqueness.

We need to be sure we are placed within a spiritual family where we can grow and support the leadership and the vision of our local church. God has called us to be committed to Him, His Word and His people in a practical way through the local church.

REFLECTION

Describe how the body of Christ is like the human body. What happens when someone is misplaced in the body? What should you do if you feel you do not fit in?

What is the Church?

+ many parts, some in leadership + some in lesser roles yet still very important. Unified + responsive in unity to one another + can be functional or dead but all needed & placed where they ought be. You might end up walking on your hands. Inquire of God + leadership + either conform submit or leave + go to another that you fit or can perform

41

Unified but not exclusive

It is important to have the same basic vision within a church family because if we do not dwell together in unity, God cannot command a blessing (Psalms 133:1-3). But we cannot be exclusive. In the book of 1 Corinthians, one of the believers said, "I am of Paul," and another said, "I am of Apollos;" another said, "I am of Cephas (or Peter)," and another said, "I am of Christ" (1 Corinthians 1:12).

Paul wrote back and told them that this was wrong. "Is Christ divided?" he asked. There can be no division in the body of Christ, neither should it be exclusive. The Lord warns us of placing one church (or one cell group or house church) as better than another. The scripture says in 1 Corinthians 12:5-6, *There are different kinds of service, but the same Lord. There are different kinds of working, but the same God works all of them in all men.*

We are called to love and encourage people from many different churches. However, we also need to be committed to and in unity with those in our church family, whether in our small group, local congregation or house church.

Sometimes believers want to change from one local church to another. If someone believes the Lord is asking him to become involved in another church, he should talk to his trusted spiritual leaders first. If there is a difficulty in his former church, he needs to go the "hundredth" mile to be sure he has a clear relationship with that church and their leadership. If he doesn't, his problem may follow him.

REFLECTION
Why is division so detrimental to the body of Christ?
Why is exclusiveness detrimental?

When our church began in 1980, we were commissioned out of our former church. Although our new church has a different "personality" than the church we were commissioned from, we still have a wonderful relationship with the precious people in our former church.

A unified church will multiply

One kernel of corn planted in a field will produce approximately 1,200 kernels of corn. If these 1,200 kernels of corn are planted the following year, they will produce 1,440,000 kernels of corn. This is called the principle of multiplication. Every church should multi-

pride slips in, blessing is cut off + the church divided

42 *falls.* *Churches need new blood* *Biblical Foundations*
+ growth being exclusive negates our commandment to spread
the gospel + evangelize — where's the love in exclusiveness.

ply. One person shares with another person the good news of Jesus. This person receives Christ into his life and shares with another. And the church grows. Growing churches start new churches!

The Lord's desire is for His church to go forth in power and authority as Christians go from house to house in every community, throughout every city, town and nation of the world. In a vision the Lord gave me many years ago, I saw missiles shooting out of our home area to the nations of the world. These missiles represented believers who were sent out to other nations to share the gospel of Jesus Christ and to plant new churches. God wants to use you in your local church to touch the world.

REFLECTION
According to Matthew 28:19-20, what is our goal and responsibility on this planet? What will happen if we fulfill that responsibility (Acts 2:47)?

Every church needs a local, national, and international vision. Churches without a mission vision will eventually stagnate. Jesus says in Matthew 28:19-20 that we should go and make disciples of all nations. That's why He left us on this planet. Years ago, our local church had the privilege of encouraging a new church to start in Nairobi, Kenya. Today they have grown to more than 50 churches in Kenya and Uganda that have a vision to reach into the nations of Africa.

God wants Christians to work together, stand together and pray together as He builds His church through small groups of believers. In small groups, Christians can be trained and then sent out as a spiritual army to take localities and the nations of the world back from the devil. Jesus Christ will continue to add to His church. The Bible says the early church was *praising God and enjoying the favor of all the people. And the Lord added to their number daily those who were being saved (Acts 2:47).*

Although God's purpose for us in our churches, cell groups and house churches is to reach people for Christ, we will experience fellowship with one another at the same time. Fellowship with others is an added blessing to those who are serving Jesus. However, may we never forget why the Lord has placed us on this earth—*to know Him and to make Him known.*

※ To disciple the nations
favor from God + growth by salvation of the lost,

Roots and the grace of God

Throughout the Bible, we see examples of the Lord asking His people to set up monuments and altars as a remembrance of the things the Lord had done. In 1 Samuel 7, the prophet set up a stone as a reminder to God's people that the Lord had helped them. The Bible tells us in Deuteronomy 4:9, *Only be careful, and watch yourselves closely so that you do not forget the things your eyes have seen or let them slip from your heart as long as you live. Teach them to your children and to their children after them.*

God was concerned the children of Israel would forget the phenomenal things He had done throughout their history. He commanded them to teach their children and grandchildren.

When you join a church family, it is important to understand its "roots." Find out why God "birthed" your church. Understanding the past will give you a clear sense of what makes your local church tick. You will see the faithfulness of God.

Ask your pastors or elders for a book or articles that were written about the early days of your church family or denomination. The history of our church family is printed in a book.[1] We encourage everyone who is called to be a part of our church family to read this book so he can understand where we've come from and what the Lord has called us to do.

Someone once said, "We build on the shoulders of those who have gone on before us." Many times mistakes are made because we have not heeded the lessons learned by our spiritual forefathers.

Although each local church needs to have a clear vision, we must remember that nothing happens except by the grace of God. The responsibility to make something happen is God's. You and I simply need to be obedient. We "plant our seeds" in faith and expect them to grow, but it is not our responsibility to make them grow. We co-labor with God for His glory.

REFLECTION
Research the history of your church family and see how faithful God has been.

God bless you as you allow the Lord to place you in His body in a way that pleases Him. Remember, it is not the church of *your* choice, but the church of *His* choice. Expect the Lord to use you as He builds His church through you from house to house, city to city, and nation to nation.

[1] Larry Kreider, *House to House,* (Ephrata, PA: House to House Publications, 1998). See page 63 for ordering information.

The Importance of the Local Church

1. **We need each other**
   a. It's hard to live the Christian life all alone. Encourage each other daily (Hebrews 3:13).
   b. Meeting together regularly as "the church" encourages and equips us to grow spiritually (Hebrews 10:24-25).

2. **The church—"called out ones"**
   a. The *church* is *people*.
   b. Christians are part of the universal body of Christ (Matthew 16:18; Revelation 5:9) and also the local body of Christ (church in their community).

3. **A baby Christian needs a family**
   a. The local church is like a support system for baby Christians who will grow up spiritually (1 Peter 2:2).
   b. Baby Christians not only need to pray, study God's Word and to share their faith with others, they also need regular fellowship with other Christians.

4. **The local church is God's army**
   a. Christians are spiritual soldiers in God's army.
      2 Timothy 2:3
   b. The local church trains us to go into the "battlefield."

5. **Fitting together**
   a. Christians are living stones built together through relationships (1 Peter 2:4-5; 1 Corinthians 3:9).
   b. Each local church of believers is a distinct "field" in the body of Christ.
   c. Within each local church, small groups of believers provide mutual support, learn to grow in God and reach out to others.

6. **The local church provides leadership and protection**
   a. The early church appointed elders to lead (Titus 1:5).
   b. These leaders provide protection and discipline. 1 Thessalonians 5:14-15; Acts 20:28
   c. The local church leaders will help in discipline and restoration of a wayward member (Matthew 18:15-17).

7. **Vulnerable without a local church**
   a. If believers find themselves no longer involved in a local church, they are vulnerable.
   b. The local church provides encouragement to face problems in life so we can stand up under them (1 Corinthians 10:13).

Spiritual Family Relationships

1. **The church is made up of family relationships**
   a. Christians are related as family (Galatians 3:26).
   b. The Lord sees you as an individual bought by the blood of Jesus. He also sees you as a part of a spiritual church family meeting in small groups and larger congregations.
   c. A larger sphere of family relationships in the church involves a church denomination or network of churches working together.

2. **Family relationships bring unity**
   a. We all need each other in the body of Christ; we are one (Galatians 3:28).
   b. Every church family has certain strengths to help the greater body of Christ.

   Ex: Methodist churches grew from John Wesley's church planting efforts. The Moravian church grew from a large missionary outreach into the nations of the world. The Charismatic movement grew from a Holy Spirit outpouring of spiritual gifts.

3. **New wineskins bring new life**
   a. There is a great spiritual crop of new believers to be harvested (John 4:35).
   b. Traditional efforts will need the help of new wineskins (new churches) to accommodate the new Christians. Matthew 9:17
   c. New wineskins—small cell groups and house churches—are often more flexible for new believers.
   d. Traditional and nontraditional churches will work together to bring in the harvest in our hometowns, our regions and our nations (Acts 1:8).

4. Meeting house to house as a family

a. The early church met house to house in small groups and in larger groups (Acts 2:46-47).

b. The church is people built together in relationship with God and each other with a common vision and purpose. Relationships are built in small groups.

5. Families are connected

a. We are "living stones" built together with other Christians. 1 Peter 2:5

b. Believers are "family members" connected in the body of Christ (Ephesians 4:16).

6. Where has God placed you?

a. God arranges us where He wants us to be. 1 Corinthians 12:18

b. You may fit best in a house church network, a community church or a mega-church. Find your niche in the body of Christ!

7. Families will multiply

a. If we "go and make disciples of all the nations" (Matthew 28:19), the church will grow and multiply (Acts 6:1,7).

b. Believers in small groups are trained to pray, evangelize and make disciples. This will lead to multiplication or "spiritual mitosis."

Who Is Watching Out For You?

1. **The importance of commitment to other believers**
   a. The early church practiced loving each other (1 John 4:7) in small groups meeting house to house (Acts 20:20).
   b. Practical Christianity happens when believers commit to meeting together to help each other grow up spiritually and reach out to their world for Jesus.

2. **Leaders give us spiritual protection**
   a. God places spiritual leaders in our lives who give us spiritual protection (Hebrews 13:7,17) from the devil who seeks to devour us (1 Peter 5:8).
   b. We should recognize and honor our leaders.
   1 Thessalonians 5:12-13

3. **Leaders help keep us on track**
   a. The early believers learned from the teaching of the church leaders (Acts 2:42).
   b. Leaders help to keep heresy from coming into the church (Acts 20:28-31).
   c. We can trust leaders who have good character and integrity in their lives (Matthew 7:15-20).

4. **Leaders equip**
   a. God releases individuals with specific leadership gifts in the church (Ephesians 4:11-12).
   b. Apostles, prophets, evangelists, pastors and teachers are responsible to equip other believers for the work of ministry.

5. Leaders lead

a. A team of leaders with one leader making final decisions is the New Testament way of leadership (Acts 21:18, James led the team as an elder).

b. Elders gave oversight to local churches; apostles had a larger sphere of influence (2 Corinthians 10:13).

6. Leaders chosen by God and confirmed by His people

a. The leaders in the early church fasted and prayed and heard from the Holy Spirit who chose Paul and Barnabas to a new work of planting churches (Acts 13:1-4). The church then sent them out.

b. Theocracy means the leadership of the church fast and pray and the Holy Spirit speaks to them about whom he is calling to leadership. The rest of the believers confirm this appointment.

Ex: King David was anointed as king but it was not until years later when he was confirmed by other leaders and the people that he became king.

7. Leaders are always servants

a. Jesus describes a great leader (Matthew 20:26-28).

b. A good leader will serve others.

c. Deacons were tested before they were set apart to serve (1 Timothy 3:10). Why must leaders be tested before leadership responsibility is given to them?

Our Commitment to the Local Church

1. **Common vision in the church**
   a. Everyone in a local church should have a common vision and walk in unity (Psalms 133:1,3b).

      Ex: Donkey and ox cannot plow together (Deuteronomy 22:10) because they move at different paces. Each church has different visions and ways of doing things.
   b. Every church should encourage believers to support and submit to the leadership in the church so everyone can be in unity.

2. **Know where you are called**
   a. Let "peace rule in your heart" concerning where God wants you be be place in the church (Colossians 3:15).
   b. God will pour His Spirit out in the last days (Acts 2:17-18) and we will need new wineskins or churches raised up to care for these believers. Connect to a church today where you can be trained, protected and available to serve others.

3. **Agreement in the local church**
   a. A church should have a statement of faith (for example, the Lausanne Covenant).
   b. A church should make every effort to keep unity (Ephesians 4:3; 1 Corinthians 1:10) so there are no divisions in the church.

4. Support your church's vision

a. We are all needed in the body of Christ. 1 Corinthians 12:14-18

b. We should know where and how we are connected to our church body.

c. When we are connected in relationship to others in the body, we will be able to support our church's vision and leadership in practical ways.

5. Unified but not exclusive

a. Unity does not mean exclusive.

b. Paul warns the church of divisiveness (1 Corinthians 1:12) but encourages all to work together without being exclusive. 1 Corinthians 12:5-6

6. A unified church will multiply

a. Every church should multiply (One kernel of planted corn multiplies and yields great crops!)

b. We should go and make disciples (Matthew 28:19-20) and Jesus Christ will add to His church (Acts 2:47).

7. Roots and the grace of God

a. Church family should know their roots (Deuteronomy 4:9) so they have a clear sense of what makes their church tick.

b. A church with a clear vision can move in the grace of God and co-labor with Him in obedience, planting seeds of faith and expecting them to grow.

Chapter 1
The Importance of the Local Church
Journaling space for reflection questions

DAY 1

Why do we need to be connected to believers in the local church?
What does Hebrews 10:24-25 say we should spend time with other believers?

DAY 2

What is the church? What is the universal church?
What is the local church?

DAY 3

What are the four things a spiritual baby needs in order to grow spiritually? What does our heavenly Father call us (2 Corinthians 6:18)?

Biblical Foundations

DAY 4 *Why must we be like soldiers? Who are we fighting (John 10:10)?*

DAY 5 *How are you God's field and building (1 Corinthians 3:9)?
Do you know where you fit into God's kingdom?*

DAY 6 *What are some things spiritual leaders provide in the local
church (1 Thessalonians 5:14-15)?*

DAY 7 *Why are we vulnerable without a local fellowship of believers to
support us?*

Chapter 2
Spiritual Family Relationships
Journaling space for reflection questions

DAY 1

Describe the way your local group of believers is related to other groups. Do you feel like a part of the church family?

DAY 2

Why is it important to recognize we need each other in the body of Christ? Why do local churches need to be in relationship with other churches?

DAY 3

Who are those "ripe for harvest" (John 4:35)? Why are new wineskins important to new Christians?

How did the early church come together (Acts 2:46-47)?
What happens when people are built together in relationship?

From what is the church called out?
How are we connected as a family?

Why does God want us in a particular place in His church
(1 Corinthians 12:18)? What other options, beside the more
traditional community church or mega-church, are there for you
to experience "church"?

Explain the principle of multiplication. What had to be spread
before the church could multiply in Acts 6:1,7?

Chapter 3
Who is Watching Out for You?
Journaling space for reflection questions

DAY 1

How is a small home group a great way to promote true fellowship? How have you helped to meet the needs of others in your small group?

DAY 2

List ways your spiritual leaders have watched out for you.

DAY 3

Why is heresy so devastating to a church? How do we keep from heresy, according to Acts 2:42?

DAY 4 *Name the five ministry gifts given to the body of Christ. Have you been equipped and released in a particular gift so that you can minister to others?*

DAY 5 *According to Acts 15, how did the early church model the fact that team leadership is more effective than one single person leading alone? Why is it important to have clear leadership for a team?*

DAY 6 *What does church government by theocracy mean?*

DAY 7 *How was Jesus the model for servant-leadership? Why must leaders be tested before leadership responsibility is given to them?*

What is the Church? 59

Chapter 4
Our Commitment to the Local Church
Journaling space for reflection questions

How does your personal vision compare with your church's (or small group's) vision?

According to Colossians 3:15, what is the basic evidence that you are where God wants you to be?

What is your responsibility in keeping unity in your small group, your church, your family? Why is it so important for believers in a local church to agree (1 Corinthians 1:10)?

DAY 4 *Describe how the body of Christ is like the human body. What happens when someone is misplaced in the body? What should you do if you feel you do not fit in?*

DAY 5 *Why is division so detrimental to the body of Christ? Why is exclusiveness detrimental?*

DAY 6 *According to Matthew 28:19-20, what is our goal and responsibility on this planet? What will happen if we fulfill that responsibility (Acts 2:47)?*

DAY 7 *Research the history of your church family and see how faithful God has been.*

What is the Church?

Daily Devotional Extra Days

If you are using this book as a daily devotional, you will notice there are 28 days in this study. Depending on the month, you may need the three extra days' studies given here.

Be a Good Minister

DAY 29

Read 1 Timothy 4:6,10. Suppose you are called to be a leader of a cell group or leader of a church. How would you know what God wants you to do? What would your vision or goal be? Who could help you?

A Worthy Workman

DAY 30

Read 2 Timothy 2:15. What scriptures stand out from these studies of the local church that have changed your life. How?

Keys to the Kingdom

DAY 31

Read Matthew 16:16-18. Review the "rock" on which Christ is building His church. Can you confess with Peter, "Jesus is the Christ—the Son of the Living God"?
What does the Lord promise us in these scriptures?

Biblical Foundations

Coordinates with this series!

Biblical Foundations for Children

Creative learning experiences for ages 4-12, patterned after the *Biblical Foundation Series*, with truths in each lesson. Takes kids on the first steps in their Christian walk by teaching them how to build solid foundations in their young lives. *by Jane Nicholas, 176 pages:* $17.95

Other books by Larry Kreider

Hearing God 30 Different ways

The Lord speaks to us in ways we often miss. He has many ways of speaking, including through the Bible, prayer, circumstances, spiritual gifts, conviction, His character, His peace, and even in times of silence.

30 ways in 30 days Take the next 30 days, reading a chapter each day, to explore ways God speaks. Expect to be surprised! Use as a personal devotional or go through this material with your small group or congregation. *by Larry Kreider, 224 pages:* $14.99

The Cry for Spiritual Fathers & Mothers

Returning to the biblical truth of spiritual parenting so believers are not left fatherless and disconnected. How loving, seasoned spiritual fathers and mothers help spiritual children reach their full potential in Christ. *by Larry Kreider, 186 pages*: $11.95

The Biblical Role of Elders for Today's Church

New Testament leadership principles for equipping elders. What elders' qualifications and responsibilities are, how they are chosen, how elders are called to be armor bearers, spiritual fathers and mothers, resolving conflicts, and more. *by Larry Kreider, Ron Myer, Steve Prokopchak, and Brian Sauder.* $12.99

Visit www.h2hp.com for more information

Hearing God 30 Different Ways

Learn to "tune in" to God and discern "HIS" voice. God wants to speak to you. Includes a seminar manual.

Spiritual Fathering & Mothering Seminar

Practical preparation for believers who want to have and become spiritual parents. Includes a seminar manual.

Elder's Training Seminar

Based on New Testament leadership principles, this seminar equips leaders to provide protection, direction and correction in the local church. Includes a seminar manual.

Small Groups 101 Seminar

Basics for healthy cell ministry. Session topics cover the essentials for growing cell group ministry. Each attendee receives a *Helping You Build Manual*.

Small Groups 201 Seminar

Takes you beyond the basics and into an advanced strategy for cell ministry. Each attendee receives a seminar manual.

Counseling Basics

This seminar takes you through the basics of counseling, specifically in small group ministry and others. Includes a comprehensive manual.

Marriage Mentoring Training Seminar

Trains church leaders and mature believers to help prepare engaged couples for a strong marriage foundation by using the mentoring format of *Called Together*. Includes a *Called Together Manual*.